Edited by **Bettina Havig**.
Designed by **Emily Sheeder**.

ISBN: 0-9676310-3-3
Printed in Korea.
First Printing: 2002

Published by
Fons & Porter, LLC.
P.O. Box 171
Winterset, IA 50273
515.462.1020
www.fonsandporter.com

Fons&Porter's

Quilt Tip *a day*

PERPETUAL CALENDAR

Dedicated to TV tipsters nationwide.

Make a New Year's resolution

to make at least one more quilt next year

than you did this year.

Tip Categories

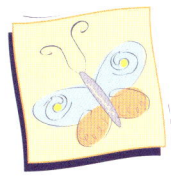

appliqué, hand or machine, including fusing tips

binding, cutting and application

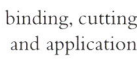

construction, layout, quilt designing

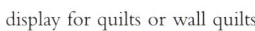

display for quilts or wall quilts

fabric, fabric preparation, etc.

gift ideas

ironing or pressing

labels for quilts, writing on quilts

miscellaneous tips

Before rotary cutting, spray limp fabrics with

starch or spray sizing to firm them up.

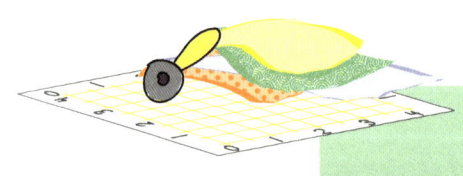

 piecing, both hand and machine

 sewing machine use and care

quilting, both hand and machine

tools, new tools, substitute tools

 rotary cutting, rotary cutters, mats, and rulers

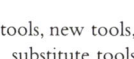 threads, threading, care of threads

work space ideas including areas not necessarily in the sewing room

reference, future ideas, books, records of quilts

 storage ideas for quilts, tools, or fabric

 workshop needs and things to take along

Try using fabric adhesive spray to baste together

the layers of a quilt or to temporarily position

appliqué pieces before stitching.

J A N U A R Y 1

Store the templates, cut fabric pieces,

and instructions for a block in a

three-ring transparent sheet protector.

When the project is completed,

file the sheet protector in a binder

for future reference.

When you sew a pillow cover or other

envelope of fabric that must be turned and later

closed, leave a long tail of thread from the machine

where you end stitching. Use this thread to hand

stitch the opening closed.

When using yarn, crochet cotton,

or other heavy threads, cut the leading end of

thread at an angle. Place the end of the yarn into

the crease of a narrow strip of paper.

Use the creased paper to guide the yarn through

the eye of the needle.

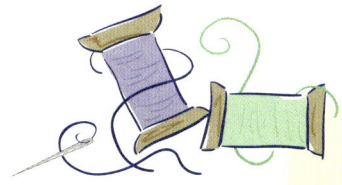

To relax the wrinkles in a polyester quilt batt, open and unfold the batting and briefly warm it with your hair dryer. The wrinkles will vanish.

After using a seam ripper to break every third

or fourth thread, apply a strip of tape to the

loose threads. Run your finger or thumb over the

tape as if finger pressing. Pull the tape up. All the

thread ends are pulled up with the tape.

Spray starch and press the fabric before tracing

redwork or other embroidery designs onto it.

Tracing will be easier, and the lines not completely

covered by embroidery will be easier to remove.

To help keep track of your needle while

working, cut a short piece of peel and stick

craft magnet. Attach the magnetic strip to the

top of the spool of thread. Keep your needle on the

magnetic strip. It won't roll off and will

be ready when you need it.

As you take workshops next year, make sample

blocks from Christmas fabric. You can then assemble

them into Christmas pillows, wall quilts, or a

sampler to give as gifts next Christmas.

Use a magnetic pin holder to locate pins

or needles lost in the carpet. Invert it and scan the

floor area where the pins may be hiding.

Use an ultra-fine steel crochet hook to

fish out a wayward dark thread from between your

quilt top and batting.

As you complete a project, take a photo,

record the pertinent information

(including the recipient if a gift),

and put the information into a photo album.

Fold an old twin-size sheet in half and

stitch on two sides to form a giant sack. Put the tail

of your quilt into the sack to keep your quilt clean

and out from under foot while quilting.

Your bagged quilt will also be easy to store away

or take with you on trips.

When working on a project that requires

many strips of fabric, stand a cardboard folding

cutting board on edge like a folding screen.

Distribute the strips over the top edge so they are

easily accessible. Fold with the strips still in place

and stand against the wall until the next use.

Use a walking foot when machine stitching the binding on your quilt. This even-feed presser foot will help keep the layers from creeping and puckering.

An over-the-door Christmas wreath holder

makes a great hook for storing various

sizes of quilting hoops.

The zippered plastic bags that some linens come in make great project bags. Do not use for long-term storage of textiles since the fabric can't "breathe."

Use a long handled paint roller with
double stick tape or reversed masking tape wrapped
around it to reach and pick up loose threads and
snippets from a fully spread-out bed-sized quilt.

Stick straight pins or safety pins into a bar of soap

to help keep them sharp.

The little plastic tripod included with
a delivered pizza will hold thread and bobbins for
storage while you work. Invert the tripod,
and put spools or bobbins on the spindles.

Advertising magnets, especially magnetic business

cards, make good substitutes for a pin grabber.

When transporting supplies to a workshop,

try slipping your rotary cutting mat and long rulers

into a standard pillowcase. It will hold both without

allowing them to bend or flex too much.

To set crayon on fabric, place a layer of wax paper atop the design and press. Protect your iron with brown paper or newsprint used as a press cloth.

To keep track of and avoid duplicating your
quilting books, record the title and authors in a
small address book. Tuck the book into your purse
for a handy reference when shopping.

Various size paper sticky dots can be used for templates for small circular appliqué shapes. Stick the dot to the fabric as a pattern; add seam allowances when cutting fabric. After cutting, remove and reposition the dot with sticky side up. Turn under the seam allowance and stick to the back of the dot. After stitching the circle in place, cut a slit in the back of the appliqué background fabric to remove the paper dot.

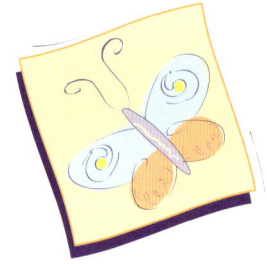

Reclaim that old folding cardboard

cutting board to use as a

portable pin-up design surface.

Cut the background fabric block for appliqué 1" larger than the desired finished block size. This will allow for "shrinkage" while you work. When you trim the background fabric to size, you can re-center the work if needed.

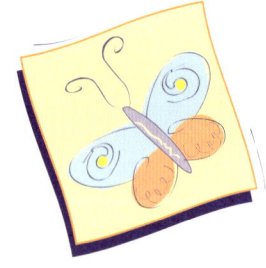

Install a plastic tie rack in your

sewing room or studio to hold cut strips

neatly sized and ready to use.

A small piece of self-sticking foam

inside your thimble helps create a snug

but comfortable fit.

J A N U A R Y   15

Place an old pillowcase over

your ironing board to protect the cover

when using fusible webbing.

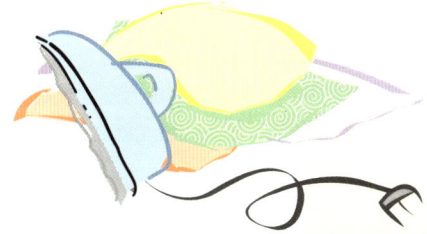

Draw or trace designs that you want to trace onto fabric onto the shiny side of freezer paper with a permanent marker. Press the freezer paper to the wrong side of the fabric to stabilize the fabric. Trace the design onto the fabric. If necessary, use a light table to make it easier to see the design through the fabric.

Look for appliqué pattern ideas in scroll saw
pattern books. You will find both plain and fancy
designs with clean, uncomplicated outlines.

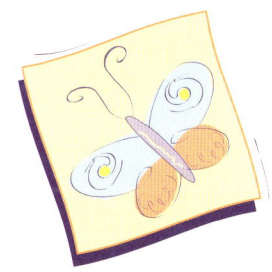

Keep an inexpensive pair of bright-handled

children's scissors next to your sewing machine

for snipping threads. If the family borrows

them, you won't care.

Store fabric pieces in special zip-top
plastic vegetable storage bags. The bags store flatter
because they have small perforations that allow
contents to "breathe" and expel trapped air.

Try the small seam roller used for hanging

wallpaper to quickly "finger-press" seams.

To stabilize fabric to make writing

on it easier, place strips of masking tape on the

wrong side of the fabric just under

the area where you will write.

Mark long sashing strips with placement lines

to align rows of blocks.

Before you prewash fabric,

snip the selvage corners off. The snips help reduce

raveling and remind you later that the fabric has

been prewashed and is ready to use.

Never make a quilt to match carpet

you don't like. The carpet may be worn out before

you finish the quilt!

Use the burn test to determine if

a fabric is cotton. Cut a snippet, and then use a

match to burn the fabric. Cotton will turn to ash;

polyester will melt. Perform the test over the sink

or other safe place.

Make your own note cards by decorating

card stock with fused on appliqués or motifs cut

from printed fabric.

Nothing is too small to be useful.

Use tiny scraps of fabric to stuff toys or pillows.

DECEMBER 8

Use empty 35mm film canisters to store

4 or 5 bobbins.

To make tracing a pattern from a book easier,

use a warm, dry iron to lightly press a

piece of freezer paper directly onto the page.

The paper won't shift or slide, and you can

see clearly. The freezer paper will peel right off

without leaving any residue.

When you have washed and ironed new cotton

fabrics, lay them over something flat like a bed,

a table, or the ironing board for 24 hours.

Cotton is very slow to completely dry. This delay

in putting the fabric away will result in fewer fold

lines and creases when you store the fabric.

Use a refrigerator magnet to pick up and

hold the blade from your rotary cutter

when you change blades.

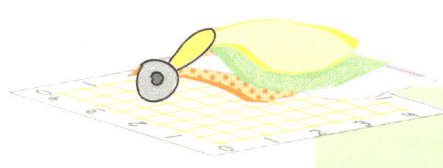

If you are having difficulty seeing clear

monofilament thread when threading your needle,

run the end of the thread across a permanent

marker. This will color only the end of the thread

and make it easier to see to thread the needle.

Simplify the cutting for continuous binding by
doing most of the cutting before joining the seam
that completes the tube. Measure the desired
widths, and cut to within about 1" on each end.
Join the fabric into a tube and finish cutting.

Many photocopy machines produce copies that may be used as hot iron transfers. The copy will transfer when ironed, but only for the first hour or so after the copy is made. The transferred lines are not permanent so you may find this a helpful way to transfer a quilting or appliqué motif.

When drawing around templates,

place a sheet of fine sandpaper under your fabric

to prevent slipping. Secure sandpaper to the table

top with masking tape.

For a quick sleeve for hanging a quilt for display,

cut the wide hem from an old, worn sheet.

Cut the tube 2" shorter than the quilt width.

Hand stitch the hem tube to the upper edge of the

back of the quilt. Use the rest of the sheet to make

a storage bag for your quilt.

To hang a wall hanging on the side of your refrigerator or other metal surface, attach a strip of magnetic tape to the slat or rod used inside the hanging sleeve. The slat or rod can be used with several different wall hangings.

To create corner holes in plastic templates that include the seam allowance, heat the end of an ice pick or a tapestry needle held in a piece of cork in the flame of a candle. Push the hot point through the plastic template to make a hole indicating the corner matching points of the seam lines.

To keep track of your quilting needle

when you interrupt your quilting, keep a

colorful piece of ribbon handy to attach to the spot

where you stopped. It's easy to locate when

you resume quilting.

Score the paper backing on fusible web

with a straight pin to

make the backing easier to remove.

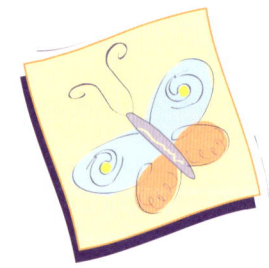

When safety pin basting, use a
crochet hook or a grapefruit spoon to help catch
the points of the pins as they emerge from under
the quilt. These tools save your fingers and help
close the safety pin.

Some dental floss is packaged in jumbo lengths

in plastic barrels. A large spool of quilting thread

will fit into the empty barrel. Thread it through

the dispenser, and use the cutter to cut

the length you need.

Insert a dime into the tip of your leather thimble

to help protect your finger.

When machine stitching through a slippery or
unruly fabric, try putting a piece of tissue paper,
like the tissue in a dress pattern, under the fabric.
You will be surprised how much easier the fabric
will move under the presser foot. Tear away the
tissue after stitching is complete.

For smooth edges on a quilt label,

pin the label right sides together with a piece of

muslin or lightweight interfacing.

Machine stitch around the label. Cut a slit in the

center of the lining, turn the label right sides out

though the opening, and press. Hand stitch the

prepared label to the quilt.

Instead if discarding large used
mailing envelopes, punch holes along one edge
to fit a three-ring binder. Use the envelopes to store
patterns and templates. Attach a photocopy or
sketch of the block or project to the outside
of the envelope so you can quickly
identify the contents.

JANUARY 31

To test to be sure your marking pencil

is removable, mark on the selvage of the fabric

before you prewash. If the mark is gone after

washing, you know the pencil is safe

to use on that fabric.

You won't feel guilty about the time and money

you spend on quilting if you get your spouse

interested in a hobby that requires at least a much

time and money. Hunting, collecting antique cars,

and woodworking are all good options.

Before chain piecing many pieces together,

fold down the top of a large grocery sack and

masking tape the wider side of the sack to the back

of your sewing machine. As you chain piece,

the pieces will collect in the sack.

You can make a combination thread holder
and cutter by winding your thread onto a bobbin
and putting it into a small, empty dental
floss holder. Pull out the thread, and cut it with the
floss cutter. We bet this will even pass airport
security so you can sew on the plane.

Thread several needles onto the spool of thread

when you sit down to work. As you empty one

needle, another will be ready to use.

To raise rectangular tables like those you

find in schools and churches to a comfortable

height for cutting, extend the legs by slipping

them into 10"–12" lengths of 2"-diameter

plastic plumbing pipe.

To clean permanent marker from

the edge of your ruler, use a cotton ball

dipped in rubbing alcohol.

Stop your family from carelessly using your

good sewing shears without your permission by

slipping a combination padlock through the

handles of the scissors.

Pin appliqué elements to the

background fabric from the back instead

of the front. The thread will be less likely to

catch on the pins as you stitch.

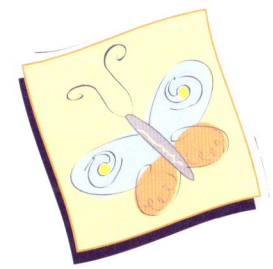

Roll a lint roller over the surface of your cutting

mat for a quick clean up.

If you find rubber fingers uncomfortable to wear

or cumbersome when you work, try a fingertip

moistener found in office supply stores. Just a touch

on the end of your finger will enhance traction for

sorting and picking up fabric pieces.

Use the front of a men's old button-up shirt for the back of a pillow. Size the shirt to the correct measurement, remove the pocket, and join to the pillow front so the buttons face out. The button placket will make it easy to insert a pillow form.

To help prevent sore fingers when quilting,

try this remedy. Apply a little Nuskin®

liquid bandage to the end of your finger.

Press on a little dab of cotton ball and then more

liquid bandage. The combination stiffens to an

almost cast–like hardness.

When prewashing fabrics, completely unfold the
fabric before putting it into the washing machine.
This will help prevent fading on the fold line and
help eliminate the strong, center fold crease.

When making continuous bias binding,

slip the fabric tube over the end of an ironing

board. You can cut the bias with one hand as you

turn the tube with the other.

Label your tools, rulers, cutters, mats, etc. with

self-stick address labels so you can tell your tools

from those that belong to others at a workshop.

Make attractive note cards with your
fabric scraps. Use purchased cards with cut-out
windows, or cut your own windows.
Insert string-pieced fragments or miniature
quilt blocks. Consider making a matching card
when you give a quilt as a gift.

To keep your rotary cutting ruler from slipping, dab clear nail polish on the under side of the ruler in a few places and sprinkle with table salt. Let the polish dry, and blow away the excess salt.

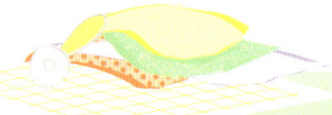

To save time when preparing for workshops,

make a permanent class kit. Put all the basic,

essential tools or supplies into it. Just grab the kit

when heading out to a workshop.

Start an index card file of your quilt magazine subscriptions. Include the date of last renewal and the issue number of the last issue due to you so you will know when you need to renew your subscriptions.

Slip a protective rubber tip made for knitting

needles over the tip of your good, small embroidery

scissors when you travel. The rubber tip will protect

the points of the scissors and you!

Keep a 6" cutting mat and small rotary cutter

by your sewing machine to clean up edges

and trim corners.

As you purchase new fabrics,

cut a small swatch from each. Glue the swatches in

a purse-size spiral notebook. Record where and

when you bought the fabrics. Take your little book

along when fabric shopping.

If your rotary cutter blade has a slight nick

on the edge and skips a few threads with

every turn, try turning the blade over with the

other side up. Often only one edge is nicked.

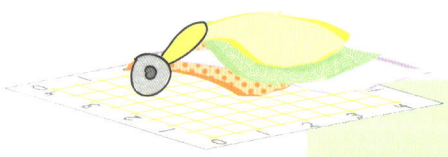

Use the end of a balloon

over your index finger to help pull through

stubborn stitches when hand quilting.

Before using x-ray film for templates,

soak the film in straight bleach to clear the film and

lighten the darkened areas.

Slip a rubber finger guard from an

office supply store on the finger under the quilt to

protect your fingers when hand quilting.

Guards are inexpensive so don't worry if

they wear out quickly.

Take graph paper or a small graph paper pad with you to quilt shows, guild meetings, and workshops so you can easily sketch block designs.

Attach a short strip of wide masking tape with

sticky side up near your quilting frame

or sewing machine. As you snip short lengths

of thread, put them on the tape for easy clean up.

Use permanent fine-tip pens to trace
designs for embroidery. Use red for red embroidery,
blue for blue, green for green, and so on.
Your stitches will cover and conceal the tracings,
and if you miss a stitch, it won't show.

Use a serger with the needles unthreaded
to cut bias for binding. After making the
usual tube for continuous bias binding, place the
beginning cutting line along the serger knife.
As you run the serger, keep the cutting line
even with the blade.

Take a pair of white gloves along to

quilt shows. With permission, you may be allowed

to touch the quilts.

Use a Polaroid® camera or digital camera

to capture various setting ideas for quilt blocks.

You can then use the photo record to compare the

settings and choose the one you like best.

Before washing small fabric pieces, put them into a

mesh laundry bag to reduce fraying and tangling.

After joining opposing patchwork seams,

remove the last one or two stitches in the

seam allowances. Open the seams down to the line

of stitching at the intersecting point, and press the

seam allowances in opposite directions to create

smoother patchwork. You can often separate

the seams without clipping.

Attach a heavy-duty, felt furniture protector to

the top of your spool of quilting thread. It makes a

great place to park your needle.

To help hold the edge of your quilt in a Q-snap®

frame when quilting borders, slip a knit rolling pin

cover or sleeve over the bar of your frame.

Pin the edge of your quilt to the sleeve to

keep the tension right.

Buy yourself a 120"-long dressmaker's tape to use

for measuring your quilt top for borders.

To help pull through stubborn needles

when hand quilting, cut a finger tip from a pair of

old rubber gloves. Slip the glove finger tip over

your index finger. The finger tip grips the needle

well and helps relieve thumb fatigue.

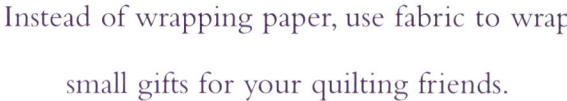

Instead of wrapping paper, use fabric to wrap

small gifts for your quilting friends.

They will appreciate the bonus gift, and the

cost is not much more than wrapping paper.

Tie the packages with selvages or narrow

fabric strips instead of ribbon.

Stick the felt dots sold to protect furniture

onto the underside of your rulers to keep them

from slipping on the fabric as you rotary cut.

Use selvage strips or other skinny,

leftover fabric strips in the garden to tie up

tomato plants, branches of fruit trees, or hang on

shrubs to deter deer. The fabric is gentle on the

plants and biodegradable.

Cut up plastic milk jugs for inexpensive,

plastic template material.

Create a safety guard on your rotary cutting

ruler by gluing the clear plastic corner protectors

used to protect wall paper about ¾" in from

the edge of your ruler.

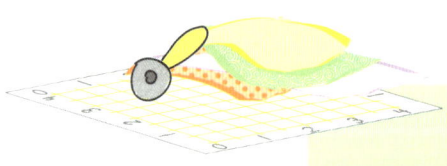

Use x-ray film to make

heat–resistant templates that you can press the fabric

over to prepare appliqué pieces.

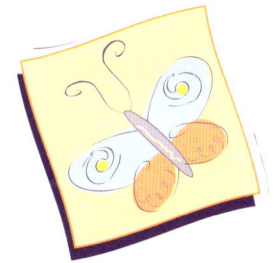

Use a sticky note to remind yourself of the machine

settings you are using for a project. When you

return and turn the machine on again, the note will

remind you which foot, needle, thread, setting, and

tension you had been using.

Use a soldering iron to

perforate plastic template material to make stencils

for quilting designs.

Cut a rubber bathtub mat to the size of your

machine foot control. Place the mat under the foot

control to keep it from sliding as you work.

In place of a stiletto, which might damage your

sewing machine if the needle hits it,

use a bamboo skewer to feed the patchwork

through the machine.

Clear plastic sheet protectors are a handy way to store quilt patterns and templates. Keep them nice and flat in a loose leaf notebook.

To get the perspective of distance

on a quilt plan, view it through a door peephole

insert from the hardware store.

This inexpensive gadget can help you "read" how

fabrics will look from a distance.

To help support a quilt when machine quilting,

place your ironing board next to your sewing

machine and adjust it to machine height.

When you clean and oil your

sewing machine, work over a large cookie sheet

lined with a white towel or paper towel.

If you drop any small screws or parts they will

show up on the white towel.

An empty Chap Stick® tube, lipstick tube,

or 35mm film canister is a safe receptacle for used,

ready-to-discard needles.

Use a soft foam ear plug to secure the thread

on a spool. Draw the loose end of thread across the

hole in the spool, and push the foam ear plug into

the hole to secure the thread.

If you didn't allow enough thread to end

hand stitching or quilting, change to a

self-threading needle. Insert the needle for the

final stitch, thread the self-threading needle,

and end your line of quilting.

Use baking parchment paper to
help you position and align appliqué pieces
prepared with fusible web. Place the appliqué
pattern under the translucent parchment paper,
position all the pieces, and fuse to the
parchment paper. When the paper cools, peel up
the entire appliqué design and fuse it as one piece
to your background block.

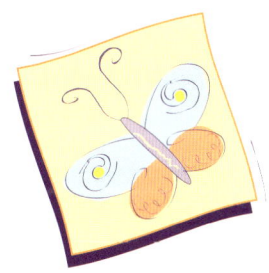

After threading your needle, give the thread a quick

pull or snap to help avoid tangling and twisting.

For projects with bead embellishments,
use a seven-day pill holder to keep beads separated
and to keep them from spilling. Close off some
sections, and use your needle to pick up beads
from the open sections.

Use large paper clips to hold your binding in place

while hand stitching it. The thread is less likely to

catch on the paper clips than on pins.

Keep empty waxed paper or aluminum foil boxes to store blocks for a quilt in progress. Carefully remove the serrated cutting edge from the box, roll blocks onto the empty tube, and store. Rolled blocks won't get sharp fold lines as when folded. Don't use for long-term storage because the acid in the cardboard may discolor the fabrics.

When changing thread on your sewing machine, cut the thread at the spool, and pull the thread out toward the needle. This will avoid fuzzing up the tension disks and will actually "floss" the tension mechanism at the same time.

Lower the sewing machine feed dogs when

changing presser feet to reduce the risk of damage

to the feed dogs and to make it easier to

change presser feet.

To protect your long rotary cutting rulers when traveling, sandwich them between discarded cardboard cores from fabric bolts. Hold the sandwich together with heavy rubber bands.

Turn your ironing board around

and use the square end for pressing

a finished quilt top.

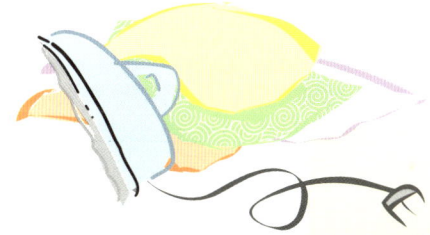

When using plastic zip-top storage bags to

store fabrics or projects, cut a very small corner

off the bag to allow air to flow out of the bag.

The bag will store flatter, and you have less

chance of trapped moisture.

Try this trick to help press out stubborn fabric creases or folds such as the center fold. Mix a few drops of white vinegar with distilled water. Use a cotton swab to moisten the crease or fold with the vinegar mixture before pressing.

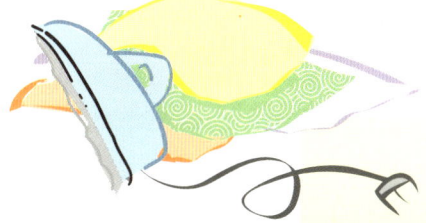

Carry your iron to workshops in a basket or metal bucket. At the end of the day, you can place the hot iron in the basket or bucket for the trip home.

Keep stacks of cut fabric pieces together
by running a length of thread up through the entire
stack. Lift off the patches as you need them.

When working with a design that requires

multiple templates which are each used only once,

cut exact finished-size templates from freezer paper.

Iron each template to the wrong side of the fabric.

Cut the fabric ¼" larger to allow for seam

allowance. Join the pieces, using the edge of the

paper as a seam guide.

Use a baby's soft toothbrush to brush away

chalk markings on your quilt.

For a flat, durable batting substitute, use a flannel

sheet. Many an antique quilt was made this way.

Fold long lengths of fabric over a

coat hanger to store them. This will help prevent

sharp creases that result from folding and

stacking fabrics for storage.

Cut unused x-ray film into 8½" x 11" pieces, and

photocopy templates directly onto the film. Be sure

to double check for pattern distortion which can

result from photocopying.

Tape a small plastic or paper bag to the edge

of your table or sewing cabinet to catch cut threads

and fabric snips.

Wrap a small piece of plastic wrap around a spool

of thread to keep the thread from unwinding.

Safety pin a 4"-6" square of low loft batting

to your shoulder to stick threads on when you are

machine piecing.

Draw your appliqué block layout or master pattern on freezer paper. Press the paper to the back of the background fabric. The design can be easily traced onto the fabric, or you can appliqué directly through the paper and remove the paper after completing the block. Make a mirror image tracing of your design if it is asymmetrical.

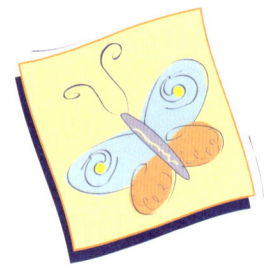

To protect the numbers and markings on your
rotary cutting ruler from wear, cover the surface
with clear contact paper. You can also make
temporary notations on your ruler by marking on
the clear contact paper.

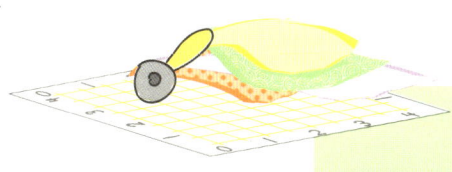

Keep a finger moistener from an

office supply store next to your sewing machine.

Moisten your finger to create a tackiness to aid in

picking up even the smallest pieces of fabric.

A medium-size tackle box with

two fold-out trays makes a great storage container

for small supplies and notions.

Before bidding farewell to that old dishwasher,

rescue the utensil basket. Use it for storing scissors,

rotary cutters, and pencils on your

cutting or work table.

The plastic tray inserts from cookie packages make excellent spool caddies and keep threads from rolling around in your drawers as well.

Store fusible web on empty rolls from foil, plastic wrap, or paper towels. Slip the roll into a zip-top plastic bag to keep the fusibles fresher.

To help keep metallic threads from separating

and breaking when hand quilting,

draw a length of thread over beeswax.

Wrap the eraser end of a pencil or small dowel with

double stick tape or masking tape, sticky side out,

and use it to pick up pieces of fabric as you work.

Used sewing machine needles make

great "nails" to hang picture frames

on the wall. The needles are strong and make

only a small hole.

Pick up spilled pins or needles easily by making an inexpensive pin and needle magnet. Glue a good round magnet disk to a paint stirring stick from a hardware or paint store to extend your reach.

Use the plastic instruction sheet rolled with fusible

web or interfacing to make a storage bag.

Fold the instructions to create small bags, and staple

the edges together along two sides. Store each

product in its corresponding instruction bag.

To create attractive storage space from a metal or plastic trash can, cut a plywood circle larger than the top of the can and put cross strips of wood on the under side to keep the top from sliding. (Discard or store the original top.) Store whatever you need to store in the can, put the new top on, and cover all with a large round tablecloth to make a great side table or bedside table.

Store extra wound bobbins on the second

spool holder if your machine has one. Bobbins are

handy when you need a replacement.

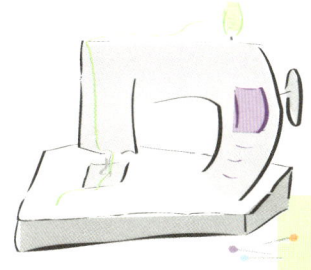

When you need an activity to occupy children,

have them draw a picture on muslin

backed with freezer paper. Heat set the crayons or

markers by pressing the fabric with a hot, dry iron.

Save the pictures to make a wall hanging or

quilt for each child.

If you are tired of turning the wing nuts

on your quilt hoop or if they no longer work,

substitute heavy rubber bands from fresh broccoli

for the bolt and nut. Just snap the rubber band

around the closure that was held by the bolt.

Store your small seasonal wall hangings

on a tube from wrapping paper that has been

covered with muslin to protect the fabric from acid

in the paper. Your wall hangings will have fewer

creases than if folded for storage.

If you use a ¼"-wide ruler to mark seam allowances,

fasten a narrow strip of 000 sandpaper to one side

to minimize slipping.

If you have accidentally fused an appliqué in the wrong place, use a fabric softener dryer sheet as a pressing cloth to loosen the web so you can remove the appliqué to reposition it.

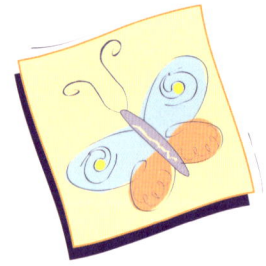

To keep track of the location of an article

or idea in magazines, photocopy the table of

contents and highlight the item you want

to remember. Keep your personal project index

in a file or notebook.

If work space is at a premium in your home, or

if you have small children, keep your rotary cutter,

mat, and ruler on top of the refrigerator.

Use a kitchen stepstool to climb up and

safely do your cutting.

If you notice a seam allowance turned

the wrong direction as you hand quilt, use a hat pin

or corsage pin to reach in and flip

the seam allowance over.

To reduce thread tangling and knotting when hand

stitching, run your unknotted thread through a

fresh, fabric softener dryer sheet a couple of times.

When making a child's quilt,

make an extra block or two to appliqué onto

pillowcases to match the quilt.

Use rubber cement to attach fine-grit sand paper

to a heavy piece of cardboard or plywood

to make a non-slip surface for tracing around

templates onto fabric.

Old-fashioned, cushioned bobby pins make great

clips to hold your binding while hand stitching it to

the back of your quilt.

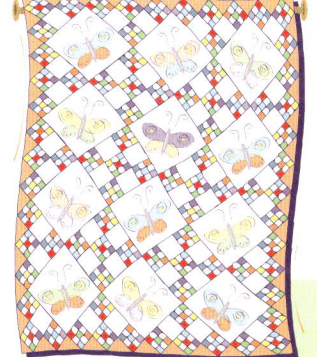

A small pillow on your lap may help put

your hand piecing or hand appliqué at a more

comfortable level.

In addition to the usual information,

transfer or print a photo of yourself onto the quilt

label as documentation. Think how much fun it will

be years later to see how you looked when you

completed the quilt.

To keep cut pieces separated into stacks by

size or color, use paper plates between the stacks.

Make pertinent notations on the plates.

Make metallic threads less likely

to separate by sliding the leading inch or so

across a glue stick.

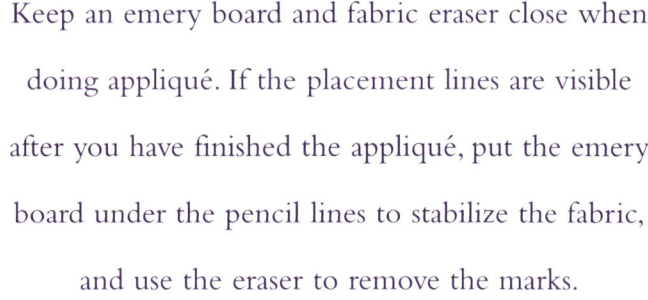

Keep an emery board and fabric eraser close when doing appliqué. If the placement lines are visible after you have finished the appliqué, put the emery board under the pencil lines to stabilize the fabric, and use the eraser to remove the marks.

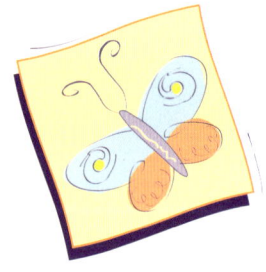

Attach the loop side of a couple of strips

of Velcro® to the bottom of your

sewing machine foot control to help it stay put

on a carpeted floor.

O C T O B E R 5

Use scraps from projects to make 6" blocks that

you can join into a pillow to fill with potpourri,

lavender, or cinnamon sticks for quick sachets.

They make great gifts or gift enclosures.

Use a little rubbing alcohol

on a cotton ball to clean your scissors blades

and rotary cutter blades.

Use a recipe file to keep a running file of magazine articles or patterns that you may want to go back to in the future. Use file tabs to keep the cards in order by category.

Safely store your rotary cutter in

an old eyeglass case.

If you like to remove the selvage edges from
your fabrics before cutting and sewing, save the
selvage strips to crochet into coasters, hot pads, or
floor rugs that are washable and durable.

If you accidentally get machine oil

on your quilt top, work some dry cornstarch into

the spots to absorb the oil. Then, brush the

cornstarch away with a soft, clean toothbrush.

When you have cut all the required pieces

for a quilt, cut the remaining fabric into strips

in widths that you know will be useful to you.

Strips widths of 1½", 2", 2½"and 4½" are

handy sizes. Store the strips folded in clear shoe

boxes labeled with the strip width so you can easily

see what you have on hand.

Avoid using fabric softener in the

washer or dryer when you prewash fabrics

that you later intend to fuse. Fusible web

will not adhere properly to fabrics treated

with fabric softener.

If you use a basting gun, try using lighting grids

for fluorescent light fixtures under the quilt

as you tack baste. The grids are usually 24" x 48"

and can be easily moved under the quilt as

the basting progresses.

The examining table paper from the

doctor's office is great for paper foundation piecing

or to use as a stabilizer for machine appliqué

or decorative stitching.

The backing for string or foundation piecing

will be ultra easy to remove if you use a paper

towel as the foundation.

A P R I L 1

It takes forever to finish a quilt

if you don't work on it!

A shot of warm breath into your

metal thimble before putting it on your finger

will make it fit better.

If you can't drop the feed dogs on your sewing machine, try placing a piece of duct tape over them. You should be able to free motion machine quilt with no problem.

Switching from machine sewing to machine embroidery usually requires more frequent bobbin tension adjustments. Purchase a second bobbin case, and leave one adjusted for sewing and the other for embroidery. Mark the outside of the embroidery bobbin case with a dab of colored nail polish or a broad-tip permanent marker to make it easy to identify.

A P R I L **3**

Use the sticky side of masking tape as a lint remover

and to remove threads from your clothing.

Use photos of your own quilts

or antique quilts to create stationery. Trim the

photos and mount them on a nice quality note

paper folded for note cards. For a fancy edge on the

cards or photos, use a scissors or rotary cutter

with a decorative cutting blade.

Attach a section of dressmaker's measuring tape to

the front of your machine with wide clear tape to

make a handy measuring guide.

Try using a small crochet hook to help remove

basting stitches from your quilt. Slip the hook end

under the stitch and pull out the basting.

A P R I L 5

If you use a rubber finger stall to help pull

stubborn stitches through when hand quilting,

turn it inside out. The bumpy surface reduces

finger perspiration, and the needle will

pull through more easily.

If you are interrupted while hand stitching,

wrap the thread around the needle in a figure eight

to maintain tension on the thread until you get

back to the work.

For the times when bike clips are too large to

hold your quilt rolled up for machine quilting,

use plastic shower curtain clips.

They are easy to use and very inexpensive.

Keep a first aid kit with adhesive bandages,

first aid cream, aspirin, antacids, and a first aid guide

in a small zip-top bag.

Take it along with your travel sewing kit.

Rubber finger cots make it easier to
pull through heavy threads used to tie comforters.
They are easy to take on and off and are available in
multiple packs of 10 or 12 for under $1.50 from
drug and discount stores.

As you attach binding, don't guess where to

stop for your mitered corner. Use ¼"-wide masking

tape to remind you of just the right allowance

for the mitered turn.

To keep track of small tools while working

on a project, wear a carpenter's apron and slip your

tools into the pockets.

When using a metallic thread for machine quilting,

thread a second thread of monofilament thread

through the same machine needle.

The monofilament thread helps keep the metallic

thread from breaking.

APRIL 9

If you sew on a Bernina® with a

presser foot lifter (free hand system), train yourself

to control the foot pedal with your left foot so your

right leg is free to operate the bar that

lifts the presser foot.

To make a dust ruffle that stays neatly in place, purchase a fitted mattress cover of the correct size. Bind the gathered edge of the ruffle with bias, and zigzag the bound edge of the ruffle to the mattress cover just where the cover drops down to the side of the box springs.

Place a small strip of non-slip rubber shelf liner

under your ruler as you cut to keep the ruler from

slipping on the fabric.

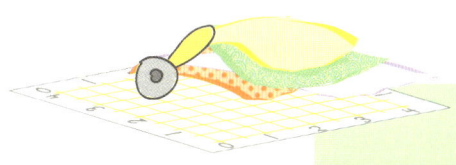

Use a banjo or guitar pick to protect your

underneath finger when hand quilting.

Use empty 35mm film canisters to
dispense thread for hand sewing. Wind 4 or 5
bobbins with the threads you need, and place them
in the canister. Puncture the lid several times,
and pull a different thread color through each hole.
You can thread needles without
the threads tangling.

If you have a tendency to lose your thimble,

drill a small hole, from the inside to the outside

near the rim. Stick a safety pin through the hole to

anchor the thimble to the quilt between

quilting sessions.

Take a wooden spring clothespin apart and use

the larger end as a "wooden iron" to press seams.

Share the other half with a friend.

To tilt your portable sewing machine toward you

for greater comfort and visibility, slip a

couple of old-fashioned rubber door stops under

the back side of the machine.

Plastic boxes for fresh berries make

handy containers for sorting small fabric squares

or other shapes.

Use a leftover party balloon as a gripper

to help pull your needle through a tough spot

when hand quilting.

Cut a small hole in the lid of an empty

whipped topping container. As you remove safety

pins from pin basting, drop them into the container.

The tight lid prevents the pins from spilling.

S E P T E M B E R   **16**

To remind you when you last replaced your

rotary cutter blade, write the date on masking tape.

Wrap the tape around the handle of the cutter.

Make a nifty wrist pincushion by

slipping a bottomless foam rubber soda can holder

onto your wrist.

Put a sticky note listing patterns and

page numbers for projects you like on the cover

of your quilt magazines.

To create a fun, all-over machine quilting design,

choose a very large scale print for your quilt back.

Motifs like flowers, fish, or animals work well.

Machine quilt from the back around the

fabric motifs. This is a great solution if fabrics on

the quilt top are difficult to mark.

Make a homemade and very portable light box

by placing an opaque white plastic storage box with

a smooth bottom upside down over a plug-in

fluorescent light strip.

To make environmentally safe spray starch,

combine 2 cups cold water and

1 tablespoon cornstarch for light starch

or 2–3 tablespoons cornstarch for heavy starch in a

spray bottle or plant mister. Since starch tends to

settle, shake well before using.

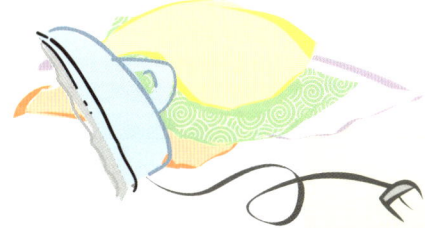

When you change machine needles, write the needle size and date on a tiny sticky note and attach it to the front of your machine. If you only use the needle for a short time, write the approximate amount of time the needle was used on the note. Poke the needle through the sticky note as you stick the needle into your pincushion.

Audition potential quilting designs

by drawing them on clear plastic. Lay the plastic

on the quilt top to get a feel for how a

quilting design will look.

Try a multiple skirt hanger to store your rotary
cutting rulers. Hang the rulers in the clips on the
skirt hangers. You can then hang the whole
apparatus over the door or on a peg.

A P R I L   **19**

Use your computer printer to make labels or print photos on cloth. Cut fabric pieces to fit through your printer, and iron freezer paper onto the wrong side of the fabric. Print the desired text or photos onto the prepared fabric. Spray printed fabric lightly with white vinegar mixed with water, and press to set. A piece of muslin or other light fabric can be used as a pressing cloth if desired.

If you display quilts on a wooden rod or quilt rack,

protect the quilt from acid in the wood by either

covering the wood with a muslin sleeve or by

coating the wood with a polyurethane finish.

Place a piece of rubber non-slip shelf liner under

your sewing machine foot control to keep it from

crawling away from you while you sew.

To make sure that the label you add to

your quilt cannot be removed, stitch it to the back

of the quilt before the quilting is completed.

Quilt through the label.

Combine three parts rubbing alcohol,

one part water, and a squirt of CLEAR dish

detergent to make a solution to remove pencil

marks from fabric. Saturate a cotton ball with the

solution and rub over the pencil marks.

When making a label for your quilt,

stabilize the label fabric with freezer paper ironed

onto the wrong side of the fabric. Drawing lines on

the freezer paper before you iron it onto the fabric

will help you write straight.

Make an extra block of each quilt you create.

When you accumulate enough blocks,

combine them into a sampler quilt as a record of

all the quilts you've made.

Use a coin, such as a quarter, as a substitute for a

wooden pressing stick to "finger press" seams.

Press a piece of freezer paper to your

ironing board cover to protect it before working

with fusible web. Remove the freezer paper and

all the fusing residue at once.

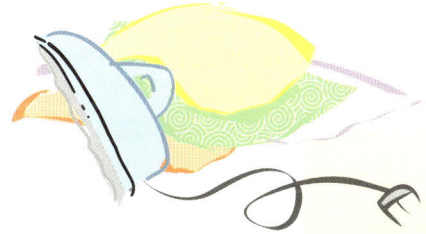

SEPTEMBER 7

The selvages that you remove from your

fabrics can double for twill tape to stabilize inside

seams of knit garments.

If you don't want to mark designs for

machine quilting on your quilt top, draw the

designs on tissue paper. Pin the paper to the quilt.

Machine quilt through the paper; then,

tear away the paper.

Saturate tiny fabric pieces for miniature quilts

with spray starch and press to make

the pieces easier to sew.

Store rolls of masking tape in a

zipper-type plastic bag. The tape is less likely to dry

out and will be easier to pull off the roll.

A new pizza box is a great way to store and
transport stacks of quilt blocks. They will stay nice
and flat. Be sure to label the box so it and your
blocks are not accidentally discarded!

To make removing paper from

paper foundation patchwork easier, dip a cotton

swab in water and "paint" the stitching lines.

Wait a few seconds, and then pull the paper away.

If the thread cutter on your sewing machine is in

an unhandy place, make yourself a substitute.

Tape the floss cutter from an empty dental floss

package into the position most comfortable for you.

To cut multiple freezer paper templates,

iron "baste" 3 or 4 pieces of freezer paper together.

Draw the pattern on the top piece. Cut through all

layers to create multiple copies.

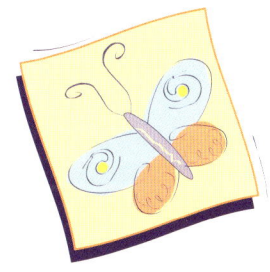

When working on an intricate appliqué design,

trace it onto clear upholstery vinyl.

Use this as an overlay to position the components

of the design. Lay the vinyl guide on top

to check the placement each time you put down a

new piece of the appliqué.

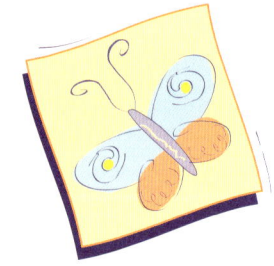

A refrigerator magnet makes easy work of

picking up pins and needles.

Use tape to guide stitching diagonal seams.
Stick the tape to the throat plate and front of the
sewing machine so that the left edge of the tape
forms a stitching guide directly in line with the
sewing machine needle. Stitch so that the corner of
the piece follows along the left edge of the tape,
guiding you along the perfect diagonal.

Place a small, table-top ironing board across the

arms of your favorite chair to make a comfortable

work space for hand stitching.

When rotary cutting around pieces which will
require turning the cutting mat, put the mat on a
Lazy Susan or other turntable. You will avoid
disturbing the fabric and maintain greater accuracy.

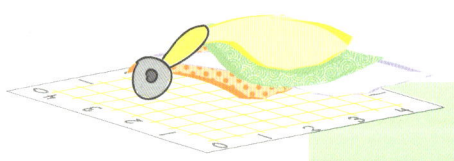

If you baste a quilt on a hardwood or tile floor,

use masking tape to secure the edges of the backing

before laying out the batting and top.

For freezer paper appliqué, try reversing the freezer

paper after using it to cut the shape.

Reposition the freezer paper with the shiny side up

on the wrong side of the fabric pieces. Iron the

seam allowance over and onto the freezer paper.

You get a sharp turned edge, and the paper can be

removed and reused. If your shape is asymmetrical,

you will need a mirror image template.

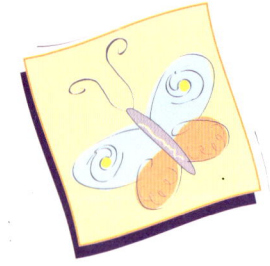

M AY 1

To make the elusive notch in a spool of thread

easy to find, mark the notch with a

permanent marker before removing thread from

the notch for the first time.

Try a curved needle for tying quilts.

The curve in the needle brings the point

of the needle back to your hand easily and

saves strain on your fingers.

Protect the tip of your scissors by

covering the tips with a length of vinyl tubing from

your local hardware store.

To make foundations for paper piecing,

make a master copy of the design. Stack the master

copy on top of a stack of blank paper.

Machine stitch through all the layers using an

unthreaded needle. Use the perforated lines to

guide your stitching as you add pieces.

The perforations will make the paper easier to

remove when the block is completed.

Make yourself a thimble with a recessed top by using an inverted wide-headed nail. Place the head of the nail on top of the thimble. Tap the point of the nail gently with a hammer to form a depression in the top of the thimble.

A U G U S T   28

When you make a baby quilt, include the name and birth date of the child as part of the label, or stitch this information directly on the quilt.

M A Y   4

Use a small piece of tape wrapped around

your finger, sticky side out, to remove stray threads

left after ripping out a seam.

When you give a quilt as a gift, include care,

washing, and storage information with the quilt.

M A Y   5

Pin a small, zipper-type plastic bag to
your quilt to store your thread, small scissors, and
other notions and to keep them from wandering
away between quilting sessions.

Put the scraps or leftover fabrics and photo

of the quilt into a plastic sleeve protector or

large zip-top bag. If the quilt needs repair, you will

have both the fabrics and the photo to

make the job easier.

For a comfortable, tight fit, coat the inside
of your thimble with "sticky stuff" used for
sorting papers. A thin coating of rubber cement
will give the same result.

To quickly determine which direction the seam

allowance is pressed when quilting in the ditch,

hold a flashlight under the quilt.

M A Y 7

For appliqué or embroidery work, keep multiple

needles threaded with all the colors you need.

You'll save time and thread.

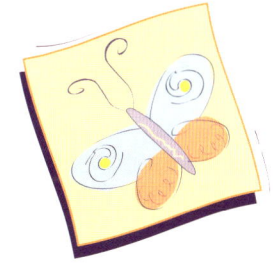

To help protect your underneath finger

when quilting, try coating the tip of your finger

with clear nail polish.

MAY 8

Write the size and type of the machine needle
you are currently using and the date you
began using it on a small piece of masking tape and
stick it to the side of your sewing machine.
Remember to use the correct type and size needle
for the job at hand and to change
machine needles frequently.

Instead of using muslin or other woven fabric

as a foundation for a crazy quilt, try substituting

nylon net or tulle to reduce the bulk and weight of

the finished project.

M A Y   9

Dental floss threaders make great needle threaders

for embroidery floss or yarn.

To nearly eliminate raveling when prewashing

fabric, use a pinking blade on your rotary cutter to

pink the edge before you wash the fabric.

Strips of self-adhesive sandpaper from the hardware

store make great non-slip aids for your rotary

cutting rulers. Cut narrow strips and place them on

the under side of the ruler.

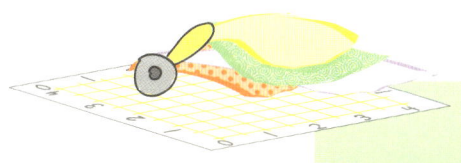

Do you ever forget that you have already

purchased a particular fabric for a project?

When you begin to plan the project, cut a 1" square

of each fabric for the project. Keep a mini file of

fabrics with you as you shop to avoid duplications.

To create a ¼" seam guide for machine piecing,

use sticky-backed mole foam cut in a narrow strip

and positioned to guide your fabric at the

correct seam width. The thickness of the mole foam

creates a ridge that the fabric slides along.

To avoid burning your fingers when pressing,

put a leather thimble on the index finger of your

hand that is not holding the iron.

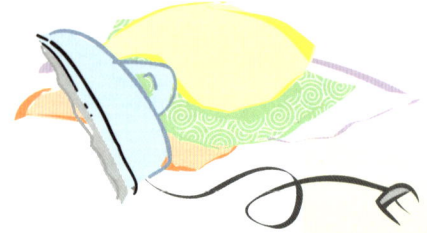

To make a thimble fit more snugly and comfortably,

wear a rubber finger tip under the thimble.

Cut the band off the rubber finger tip so it fits just

below your knuckle.

The finger tip off a pair of old leather gloves
makes a good leather thimble. A pair of old gloves
from a flea market or used clothing store will make
several usable thimbles.

Use an empty boutique-style tissue box as a
portable waste container. It's pretty, portable, and
can be at your fingertips. Even if it is accidentally
tipped over, the contents will not spill easily.

To remind yourself of the direction you want the seams to be pressed in a row of blocks, put a straight pin pointing in the direction the seams should fall. Use one pin in row 1, two pins in row 2, etc., to keep the rows in the correct order.

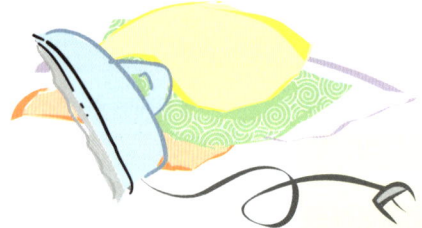

If you find a flaw in your fabric,

mark the flaw with a small brass safety pin, piece of

masking tape, or stick-on label to remind you to

avoid the flaw when cutting.

Use a dry, nylon kitchen scrubby to clean your

cutting mat. It will clean away all the lint and

threads and help heal the mat as well.

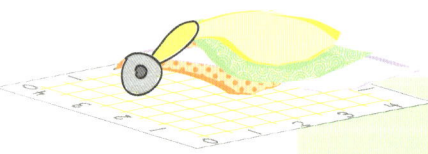

Take the time to hand baste around your quilt

before machine stitching on the binding.

This will keep the layers from creeping and

puckering as you machine sew.

A U G U S T 16

If you can't remember where you saw

that next quilt or great tip, try this.

Make a notation upside down on the edge of a

sticky note and place it on the page you want

to remember. You can see the note sticking up on

your book shelf, and the notation reminds you of

what place it marks in the book.

A small, tin throat lozenge box makes a wonderful

purse-size sewing kit. Attach a magnetic strip inside

the lid to hold pins and needles. Add a pair of small

scissors and thread, and you're set.

A U G U S T 15

Keep a chopstick handy to help turn items inside

out and get the corners nice and square.

M A Y 17

To revive brittle or dry cotton thread,

place the spool in a small, plastic bag and freeze for

a day or two. When you remove the thread from

the freezer, it will attract moisture as it thaws.

The moisture will help revive the thread.

As a gift tag for a handmade gift or quilt,

fuse a piece of leftover fabric to an index card.

Trim card to size, fold in half, punch a hole near the

corner of the fold, and put a ribbon through.

Have an extra computer mouse pad lying around?

Put it under your sewing machine foot control to

keep it from slipping on hard surface floors.

Keep an emery board in your sewing kit to

replenish the point on your marking pencil.

It will save frequent sharpening, and your

pencil will last longer.

M A Y   19

Hold a piece of white paper behind your needle

as you thread it. The paper makes it easier to see the

eye of the needle.

Use a small sticky note to mark your strip width on

your plastic ruler while rotary cutting.

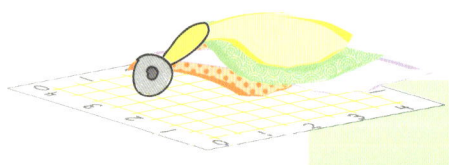

To prepare 1"-wide bias for narrow stems or stained glass appliqué, fold the bias in half, wrong sides together, and stitch with a ¼" seam allowance. Trim the seam allowance to ⅛". Slide a long, plastic electrical tie into the tube. Position the seam under the flat side of the tie, and press with a hot iron. The tie will not melt, but it will become hot, so be careful. Remove the tie before stitching the bias to the quilt.

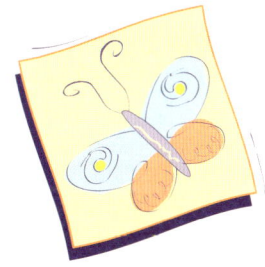

A small chalkboard or dry-erase board makes a

great place for temporary calculations while

planning, cutting, or piecing your quilt.

M A Y   21

An over-the-door, clear plastic, pocket-type

shoe organizer makes a great storage container for

your sewing area, especially if you

have limited space.

If you have a leather roller foot for your machine,
try using it for invisible machine appliqué and for
free-hand machine quilting. The roller allows
smooth movement and transitions for sharp turns
and tight curves but still regulates stitch length.

When you have a wound bobbin left and
want to remember which spool of thread it was
wound from, secure them together with a piece of
pipe cleaner or twist tie.

To save your fingers when basting, use a small spoon (a grapefruit spoon is best) on the top of the quilt. As the needle comes back through to the top, slide it into the bowl of the spoon so you can easily grab the needle.

Make the sleeve for your quilt before
you attach the binding. Catch the raw edges of the
sleeve in the seam as you machine stitch on
the binding. Secure the sleeve again as you hand
stitch the binding to the quilt back. Then, stitch the
folded edge of the sleeve to the quilt back.
This quick method is especially nice for wall quilts.

Attach a stack of several sticky notes to the

machine throat plate to create a quick seam guide

that can be quickly removed when not needed.

M A Y 24

Store your rotary cutting rulers in a

vertical desk file or letter holder so they take up

less space in your work area and you can

easily find them.

If find you need to mark quilting designs
after the quilt is in the floor frame, slide your
ironing board under the quilting frame. Adjust the
height to bring it up to the right level to create a
hard surface for easier marking.

Transfer a quilt design by first tracing the design

onto tracing or other light weight paper.

On the reverse side of the paper, retrace the design

with chalk. Position the pattern on your quilt,

chalky side down, and retrace the design to

transfer the chalk to the quilt top. Blow away the

excess chalk dust.

Place an old, worn computer mouse pad

next to your sewing machine to stick pins into,

set your scissors on, and to use as a coaster

for hot or cold drinks.

Place a small, foam-backed, carpet remnant under

your portable sewing machine to prevent sliding,

soften the noise, and protect the table top.

Tablecloth clips designed for picnic tables will help

keep fabrics smooth in preparation for

cutting or basting. They are inexpensive, flexible,

and should not mar the table.

A flannel–backed, plastic (picnic-type) tablecloth

makes a great, portable design surface.

After arranging fabric pieces, fold or roll it up,

plastic to flannel, with the project inside for storage.

No pins are needed because the fabric pieces

stay stuck to the flannel, not the plastic,

when you unroll the tablecloth.

Mount indoor/outdoor carpet to a wall to

make a design surface. You can pin into it without

piercing the wall surface.

Use a carpenter's chalk line from the hardware store to snap straight lines on your quilt. Instead of using carpenter's chalk, which is difficult to remove from fabric, use powdered dressmaker's chalk.

Identify your good scissors with a
red ribbon or yarn. Inform your family that this
indicates that these scissors are off limits.
Put a green ribbon on the scissors that
are OK for general use.

M A Y 29

Cut the bottom from a large paper grocery bag.

Slip the bottomless bag over the end of the ironing

board to protect the cover from residue from

fusible web and adhesives.

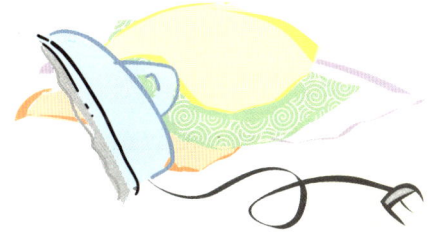

Wallet photo or I.D. holders are a great place to

keep fabric swatches to take along shopping.

The fabrics stay clean and neat.

M A Y   30

To align the quilt top, batting, and backing for basting, fold each in half and mark the center fold with pins. As you layer your quilt, match the center pins to align the layers.

Temporarily glue or tape a snip of fabric

to your template to remind yourself which fabric to

cut from the template.

M A Y **31**

Use a sliver from a bar of hand soap to mark

quilting lines. The soap lines disappear as you quilt

or wash out easily. A sliver of colored soap works

well on light fabrics.

Store a quilt in an old, white pillowcase.

Make a border to add to the case from scraps of

fabrics used in the quilt. This will tell you at a

glance which quilt is in the pillowcase.

JUNE 1

As you fill a new bobbin, stop winding
after a few revolutions. Mark the thread with a
washable felt-tip marker. Then, finish filling
the bobbin. When you see the mark, you will know
the bobbin is almost empty. No more sewing
blissfully with no bobbin thread!

J U L Y **30**

An empty, 98 oz.-size, powdered laundry detergent

box makes a perfect magazine storage caddy.

Cut away one narrow end of the box.

Leave the handle on the box for easier carrying.

Cover the box with contact paper or wrapping

paper to dress it up.

As you press continuous binding, let the binding fall into a container, such as a clean wastebasket or plastic gallon ice cream container. You can pull the binding from the container as you stitch it to your quilt without the binding tangling or twisting.

J U L Y 29

Apply moleskin to your fingertips to protect them

from needle pricks when hand quilting.

Use nail clippers to carefully remove

the plastic tacks if you've basted your quilt

with a basting gun.

J U L Y 28

Take a small paper lunch bag to a workshop and masking tape it to the table to catch all your scraps and threads. Clean up is quick and easy.

A strip of extra-wide grosgrain ribbon makes a

quick sleeve for small wall hangings. Pink the ends,

and hand stitch the ribbon edges to the back

of the quilt. Slide a small dowel through the ribbon

sleeve to hang the quilt.

A solution of ¼ cup of white vinegar per gallon of

water may help set some fugitive dyes. Soak the

fabric in the vinegar mixture for a couple of hours.

J U N E   5

Start your Christmas projects now.

To supplement the poor lighting in hotels,

bring a higher watt light bulb on trips to

temporarily replace a dim bulb.

Hot glue a small, round magnet to the top of a golf

tee. Insert the tee into the hole of a spool of thread

to make a handy place to park your needle.

J U L Y 25

To make a lightweight, portable, ironing surface,

wrap the cardboard core from a bolt of fabric with

an old bath towel and pin to secure. Great to take

to workshops because it is much lighter than

purchased lap top ironing boards.

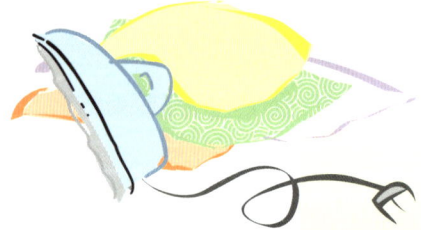

After cutting and pressing binding, roll it onto an empty cardboard tube. The binding will unroll without tangling as you attach it to the quilt.

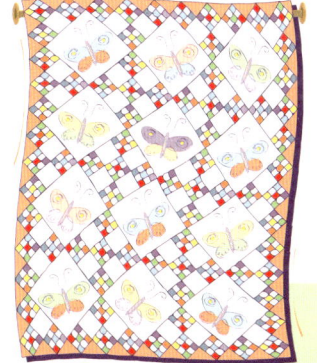

J U L Y   24

When making a baby quilt for a little girl,

make a doll quilt at the same time to give her later

to use for her dolls.

Make removing your quilt from a Q-snap® frame easier by placing 6"-8"-long strips of fabric on the quilt before you snap on the half-pipe. When it's time to reposition the quilt, pull up on the strips to pop the half pipes off and release the quilt.

J U L Y   **23**

If you have difficulty threading your needle, you

may be working from the wrong side of the eye.

Spin the needle to the opposite side and try again.

You may be surprised at how much easier it is

to thread the needle.

Instead of a wooden spool adapter for

large-holed spools of thread, use an empty, thin

plastic spool from imported thread. Cut one end off

the plastic spool and slip it inside the opening of

the larger spool.

J U L Y 22

Save the little packets of silica that

come with new shoes or other leather goods.

Store them with your needles, scissors, and pins

to help prevent rusting.

Just for fun, try binding your next scrap quilt

with a binding made from random lengths of

several fabrics used in the top.

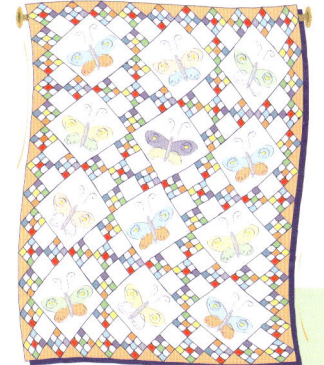

J U L Y 21

Reinforce your needle threader by dropping a
tiny drop of Super Glue® at the place where the
wire meets the disk of the threader.

Put together an emergency kit of

hand piecing that you always have in the car.

If you get stuck somewhere, you can work on this

special project. You may be amazed how soon you

complete the take-along project!

If you serge the raw edges of your fabric
before washing, you will eliminate tangles and
raveling threads.

Some quilt guilds establish a small fine for misdeeds, such as not closing your rotary cutter or forgetting your name tag at workshops and meetings. The fines accumulate to purchase something to benefit the group, such as a new book for the guild library.

J U L Y 19

When hand basting your quilt, use a spool holder to allow the basting thread to feed freely. You can pull off all the thread you need for one line of basting. Without knotting the thread, begin basting in the middle of the quilt. Pull up the first stitch so about half the thread is on each side of the stitch. When you finish basting in one direction, tie a knot in the thread. Re-thread the needle with the long thread tail to baste in the other direction.

Look through your binoculars backwards to create

a "reducing glass" to view your quilts in progress.

The binoculars give you a sense of distance from

your quilt that allows you to view the design as

a whole, rather than in parts.

For foundation paper piecing,

trace the block pattern with a transfer pencil.

You can then iron the design onto

multiple sheets of paper. Be sure the design is

symmetrical, or draw the block in reverse. You can

get 8-10 good transfers from one tracing.

Cut your binding at the same time you are

making the quilt top. Store the binding with the

quilt or in a special "binding bin" so the fabric

doesn't get used for some other project before you

are ready to bind the quilt.

If you use a wooden hoop to quilt, consider sealing

the wood with a good polyurethane finish to

protect fabrics from the acid in the wood.

If you use the large 2,500–3,000-yard spools of thread, wind several bobbins from the spool the first time you use the thread. They will be ready to go as you continue to sew from the spool.

Old coloring books are a good source of appliqué
ideas for children's quilts. Use a photocopier to
reduce or enlarge the designs. Simplify the designs
and delete details as needed.

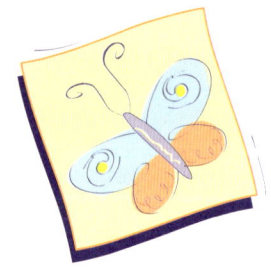

If pressing is not your favorite part of quiltmaking,

try stacking several sections. Press the seam

on the top piece. Meanwhile you will have set the

seams on the ones below.

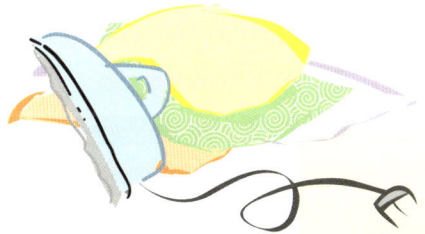

Instead of wetting the end of the thread, wet the

eye of the needle so it grabs the thread to make

threading a needle easier.

Stitch across a small fabric scrap at the
end of a seam. When you are ready to begin
stitching again, stitch off the scrap and onto the
new piece. This saves thread and helps eliminate
thread jams in the machine.

A Lazy Susan on your work table keeps

tools in easy reach.

Keep workshop handouts in a top-loading,

plastic sheet protector. Add a sample of the

technique or swatches from the fabrics used to keep

a record of the workshop. Record the date and

place you took the class.

Wrap a strip of ordinary, white adhesive tape

around the end of the finger that you

use under the quilt when hand quilting to help

protect your finger.

To wax your thread before using

for hand work, drop the spool into melted

paraffin or beeswax. The wax will saturate the entire

spool in a few minutes. Do not use this method

with a styrofoam spool.

Use vinyl floor tiles to make permanent templates

for specific size blocks. Pick up 9", 10", and 12" tiles

for quick reference.

JUNE 20

For fabrics that are difficult to mark
quilting designs on, try quilting from the back.
Frame in the area to be quilted with quilting in the
ditch so that you know where to put the design.
Mark the design on the quilt back, and quilt
from the reverse side.

J U L Y 11

Leaving even a short length of thread in your hand sewing or quilting needles will make them easier to find, especially if you accidentally drop them.

J U N E   **21**

When quilting a memory quilt,

use shapes that are meaningful to you

or the recipient. For example, use the outline of a

baby spoon or favorite small toy for a customized

quilting design for a quilt for a baby or child.

Use an old-fashioned tomato pincushion to keep

track of your machine needles.

Use a permanent pen to label each section

with the needle size or type. Put your needles into

the proper section. When a needle is in the

machine, put a long, straight pin in the tomato

pincushion in the place of the needle to remind

you which needle is in the machine.

Trace appliqué patterns onto paper;

then, laminate the paper. Cut out the laminated

pieces to use as templates.

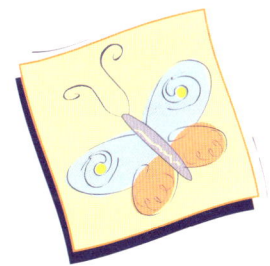

A round toothpick can help turn under

stubborn seam allowances for appliqué. If needed,

a touch of water-soluble glue will help hold the

seam allowance under.

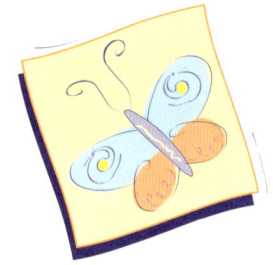

Cookie cutters make wonderful quilting templates,

especially for children's or holiday quilts.

JULY 8

Store your rotary cutting rulers on a

revolving belt holder mounted in your sewing

room or studio.

After you decide on the layout of your quilt blocks,

take a Polaroid® or digital picture to use

as a reference. Then, if you can't leave the blocks

laid out, you can refer to the picture to

remember how to arrange them.

Don't leave your rotary cutting mat in the

back of your car on a hot day.

It may permanently warp or buckle.

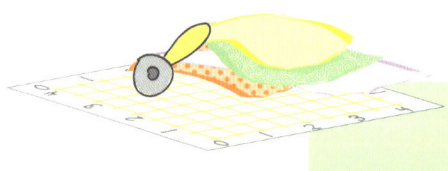

Before washing your fabric,

use a permanent marker to write in the selvage

the amount of fabric in the piece and the

intended use of the fabric.

When hand stitching the binding to your quilt back, try spring-type clothespins to hold the edges in place. Place them about 3"–4" apart.

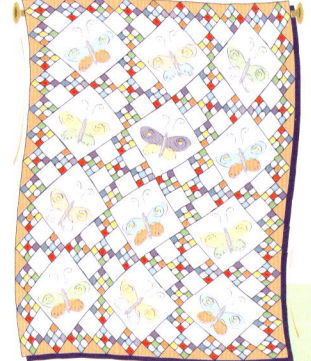

Label your blocks with row and

column information by attaching a small,

sticky label (such as a pricing label)

on one corner of each block.

JULY 5

If you pin baste for hand quilting, do it from the backing side. When you quilt, you will be less likely to snag and catch your thread on the pins.

J U N E   27

Can't find time to read and quilt?

Listen to books on tape while you stitch.

J U L Y 4

Make a red, white, and blue sampler block

when exploring a new block design.

When you have at least four blocks,

make an Americana sampler as a gift for a friend

or for yourself. Christmas fabrics make

great samplers, too.

J U N E   **28**

Use old or outgrown sweatshirts for batting

in small projects, such as placemats or potholders,

that you will machine quilt.

J U L Y   3

A fingertip moistener, available at office
supply stores, makes a great substitute for a finger
stall when pulling your needle through those
tougher spots while quilting.

Use a roll of adding machine tape to help gauge

quilting, appliqué, or patchwork designs for borders.

Measure the tape to the border length; then,

fold the tape into the desired number of repeats

for your border design.

J U L Y 2

Place a sheet of heavy-duty aluminum foil on

your ironing board under your pressing or fusing

area to reflect the heat and improve the bond.

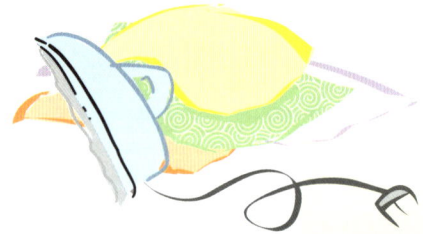

To remove fusible web residue from the bottom of your iron, place a paper towel or other paper on your ironing board. Then, iron over a fabric softener dryer sheet with a hot iron to dissolve and remove the sticky residue.

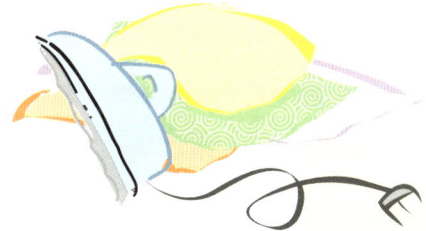

J U L Y 1

Elevate your cutting table to a comfortable

height by placing books of the same size under the

legs of the table.